Cultural Traditions in
Egypt

Lynn
Peppas

Crabtree Publishing Company

www.crabtreebooks.com

Crabtree Publishing Company

www.crabtreebooks.com

Author: Lynn Peppas
Publishing plan research and development:
Sean Charlebois, Reagan Miller
Crabtree Publishing Company
Project coordinator: Kathy Middleton
Editors: Adrianna Morganelli, Crystal Sikkens
Photo research: Crystal Sikkens
Design: Margaret Amy Salter
Production coordinator: Margaret Amy Salter
Prepress technician: Margaret Amy Salter
Print coordinator: Katherine Berti

Cover: The Giza Plateau (top center); White Ibis (top right); camel (top left); Falukas on the Nile (middle center); lotus flower blossom (middle left); baskets with spices (middle right); date fruits (bottom left and right); King Tut's burial mask (bottom middle)

Title page: Egyptians celebrate the Sham Ee Naseem festival by enjoying a donkey cart ride.

Photographs:
Alamy: Robert Harding Picture Library Ltd.: page 6
Associated Press: Amr Nabil: title page, pages 7, 8, 11, 31; Khalil Hamra: pages 20–21
Dreamstime: Wisconsinart: page 15
Keystone Press: zumapress.com: pages 12, 29; Ahmed Asad/zumapress.com: pages 16–17
Shutterstock: cover (middle center and right, top left), pages 5, 18, 20, 23; Baloncici: page 4; Attila Jandi: page 9 (bottom); Jeremy Richards: page 10 (bottom); Galyna Andrushko: page 13; Iakov Fillimonov: page 14; Ana Menendez: page 24 (right); James A Dawson: page 26 (bottom); Mohamed Elsayyed: pages 27, 28
Thinkstock: cover (all except middle center and right and top left), page 24 (left)
Wikimedia Commons: page 9 (top); B. Simpson Cairocamels: page 10 (top); Man77: page 19 (inset); Francesco Gasparetti: page 19 (except inset); Berthold Werner: page 22; Kodak Agfa: pages 25, 26 (top left); Mohamed Adel: page 26 (top right); Daniel Mayer: page 30

Library and Archives Canada Cataloguing in Publication

Peppas, Lynn
    Cultural traditions in Egypt / Lynn Peppas.

(Cultural traditions in my world)
Includes index.
Issued also in electronic format.
ISBN 978-0-7787-7517-1 (bound).--ISBN 978-0-7787-7522-5 (pbk.)

    1. Festivals--Egypt--Juvenile literature. 2. Egypt--Social life and customs--Juvenile literature. I. Title. II. Series: Cultural traditions in my world

GT4888.A2P47 2012   j394.26962   C2012-903960-8

Library of Congress Cataloging-in-Publication Data

Peppas, Lynn.
  Cultural traditions in Egypt / Lynn Peppas.
    p. cm. -- (Cultural traditions in my world)
  Includes index.
  ISBN 978-0-7787-7517-1 (reinforced library binding) -- ISBN 978-0-7787-7522-5 (pbk.) -- ISBN 978-1-4271-9041-3 (electronic pdf) -- ISBN 978-1-4271-9095-6 (electronic html)
  1. Festivals--Egypt--Juvenile literature. 2. Holidays--Egypt--Juvenile literature. 3. Egypt--Social life and customs--Juvenile literature. I. Title. II. Series: Cultural traditions in my world.

GT4888.A2P47 2012
394.26962--dc23

    2012022052

Crabtree Publishing Company

www.crabtreebooks.com   1-800-387-7650

Printed in the USA/052013/IB20130408

Published in Canada
Crabtree Publishing
616 Welland Ave.
St. Catharines, ON
L2M 5V6

Published in the United States
Crabtree Publishing
PMB 59051
350 Fifth Avenue, 59th Floor
New York, New York 10118

Published in the United Kingdom
Crabtree Publishing
Maritime House
Basin Road North, Hove
BN41 1WR

Published in Australia
Crabtree Publishing
3 Charles Street
Coburg North
VIC 3058

Contents

Welcome to Egypt

Egypt is a country with an **ancient** history and culture. People from Egypt are called Egyptians. Most Egyptians speak Arabic. Egyptians celebrate their culture with special holidays and festivals.

Egypt's capital city is Cairo. It is the largest city in Africa.

Most Egyptians practice the religion of Islam. A person who follows Islam is called a Muslim. Muslims believe in one God called Allah. They follow the Islamic holy book called the Quran. A smaller population of Egyptians follow the Christian religion and are called Coptic Christians.

Did You Know?
Islam is the official religion in Egypt. Because of this, Islamic holidays are **national** or **public** holidays. Christian holidays are not national holidays. They are only celebrated by Christians.

Muslims worship in buildings called **mosques**.

Family Occasions

Egyptians are proud of their ancient history and many **traditions** have been handed down from **ancestors** over thousands of years. Painting an Egyptian bride's hands and feet with henna the night before her wedding is believed to bring her good luck and health. Henna is a dark reddish-brown dye that lasts about two weeks.

A bride may have to sit still for hours while her female friends and family apply henna designs the night before her wedding.

Friends and family follow the seven-day-old baby with candles as its parents take it on a tour around the family home.

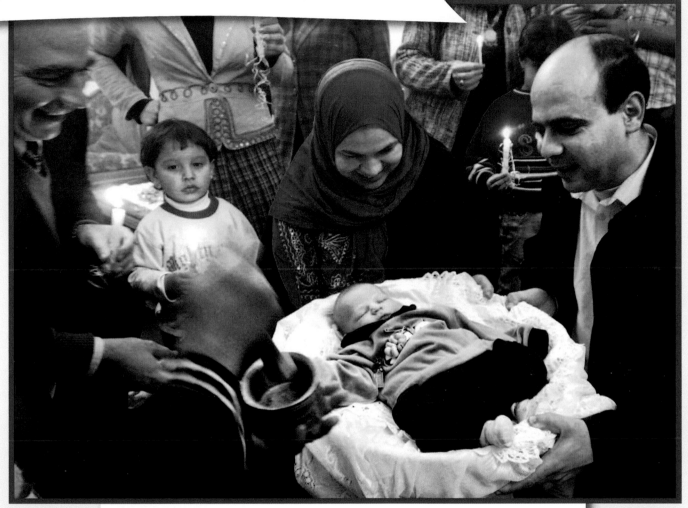

Did You Know?
Loud noises are part of the Sebou celebration. The noises are intended to make the child brave.

Egyptians believe the number seven is lucky. Seven days after a baby is born is called the Sebou. Sebou means seven in Arabic. A celebration is held with a feast, and salt is sprinkled around the house to protect the baby from anything bad happening.

Mawlid

Egyptians celebrate the birthday of the **prophet** Muhammad on the national holiday called Mawlid. Muhammad started the religion of Islam over 1,000 years ago. Muslims believe he was a messenger of God.

Did You Know?
During Mawlid, dolls and horses are popular symbols. Symbols are special figures that represent, or stand for, something else.

It is traditional for Egyptian children to receive sugar dolls and horses during Mawlid. In many places, however, plastic dolls and horses made of string have replaced the ones made of sugar.

Muhammad's face (the baby held by the angel) is almost never shown in Islamic religious pictures. This is so Muslims will not worship the image of Muhammad.

Mawlid falls on different dates each year within the third month of the **Islamic calendar**. Muslims say special prayers on this day, and cities are decorated with bright lights. In Egypt, the word Mawlid is also used for celebrations of other religious leaders and saints.

A man sells copies of the Quran, or Islamic holy book, on a street in Cairo, Egypt. The messages Muhammad received from God are written in this book.

Eid al-Fitr

Colorful lanterns help celebrate the end of Ramadan.

Eid means festival or celebration. Eid al-Fitr is one of the most important religious holidays for Muslims in Egypt. It is celebrated at the end of Ramadan, a time each year when Muslims **fast** for one month during the daytime. On Eid al-Fitr Egyptians celebrate with a big meal and desserts.

During the special Eid prayer, the Islamic religious leader says, "Allah (God) is great." When this is said, Muslims kneeling on prayer mats lean forward and touch their heads on the ground.

Many places have fairs with rides, music, and fireworks, during Eid al-Fitr.

On Eid al-Fitr many Muslims go to the mosque to pray. They give food or money to the poor. Families and friends give presents to one another. It is also a time of giving thanks and forgiving others.

Did You Know?
Eid al-Fitr is a three-day celebration. Many Egyptians enjoy time off from work or school.

11

Eid al-Adha

Eid al-Adha is an important three-day festival celebrated by Muslims. This religious holiday is also known as the Festival of Sacrifice. The holiday falls on different dates each year according to the Islamic calendar. Normally it falls about 70 days after Eid al-Fitr. Up to the year 2020, it will be celebrated in early fall.

Did You Know?
During Eid al-Adha, many Muslims make a pilgrimage, or long journey, to the Islamic holy city of Mecca in Saudi Arabia. Muslims are to do it one time during their lives.

Children enjoy buying party hats and masks to wear during Eid al-Adha.

Eid al-Adha honors the prophet Ibrahim's **obedience** to God. It is believed that God told Ibrahim to kill his young son to prove his obedience. Ibrahim was sad, but was prepared to do as God asked. God was pleased to see Ibrahim's willingness to submit to Him, so God stopped Ibrahim before he took his son's life and gave him a sheep to sacrifice instead.

Because of Ibrahim's story, Muslims sacrifice sheep, goats, or other farm animals on Eid al-Adha. They divide the meat into three parts. One part is kept for their family, one is for their relatives, and one is given to the poor.

New Year's Day

Egyptians celebrate more than one New Year's Day. In most places around the world, New Year's Day is celebrated on January 1. Egyptians celebrate this New Year's Day, but it is not a public holiday in Egypt.

Some places in Egypt celebrate New Year's Eve on December 31 with dances and a feast.

The Islamic New Year's Day is on the first day of the first month in the Islamic calendar, which is called Muharram. This religious holiday, called *El am Hejir* in Arabic, normally falls on different dates during the month of May or June. The Islamic New Year's Day is a public holiday in Egypt. All Egyptians get the day off work or school.

Did You Know?
Coptic Christian Egyptians celebrate New Year's Day on September 11 or 12. It is not a public holiday.

El am Hejir is celebrated more quietly than New Year's Day on January 1. On El am Hejir, Muslims gather at mosques to pray and listen to special readings from the Quran.

Coptic Christmas

Christmas in Egypt is a religious holiday celebrated on January 7. It is a Christian holiday that celebrates **Jesus**' birth. Even though Muslims do not celebrate Jesus' birth, the day is a public holiday for both Christians and Muslims in Egypt.

Did You Know?
Christians eat a sweet shortbread called *kaik* during Coptic Christmas. It is the same treat that Muslims prepare for their holiday of Eid al-Fitr.

Christmas Eve is celebrated on January 6 and many Christians in Egypt go to church. After church they share a meal called *fata*, which is usually lamb and rice. Presents are given and received on Christmas Day. Families and friends get together to share a turkey dinner. Many people hang colored lights and decorate their homes with Christmas decorations.

Pope Shenouda III was a leader of Christianity in Cairo, Egypt. He died on March 17, 2012. He is shown here leading his last Christmas Eve service on January 6, 2012.

Abu Simbel Sun Festival

The Abu Simbel Sun Festival is an ancient celebration that dates back over three thousand years. The ancient pharaoh, or ruler, named Ramses the Second had the Abu Simbel temple built in his honor. Statues of the pharaoh sit both inside and outside, along with statues of ancient Egyptian gods.

Four statues of Ramses that stand 66 feet (22 meters) tall guard the entrance to the Abu Simbel temple.

Seated with the two sun gods is a statue of Ramses himself and Ptah, the god of darkness.

The festival is celebrated on February 22, the day of Ramses' birthday, and October 22, the day he was crowned pharaoh. These two days are the only times of the year that the Sun shines inside the Abu Simbel temple onto the two statues of the sun gods Amun-Ra and Ra-Harkhti. Although they are not national holidays, many people still travel to Abu Simbel to celebrate these amazing events each year.

Did You Know?
The Abu Simbel temple was moved about 700 feet (213 meters) from the Nile River in Egypt in the 1960s.

Sinai Liberation Day

Sinai **Liberation** Day is a public holiday in Egypt. It celebrates the removal of Israel's army from a part of Egypt called the Sinai Peninsula. Celebrated on April 25, Egyptians get the day off of school or work.

Egyptians watch military shows to celebrate Sinai Liberation Day.

The Sinai Peninsula is an area of land that forms a bridge between the continents of Asia and Africa. The Sinai Peninsula in Egypt was captured by Israel during a war between Egypt and Israel in 1967. Over ten years later, the two countries signed a treaty and Israel agreed to give the land back to Egypt.

Did You Know?
The **peace treaty** that returned the Sinai Peninsula to Egypt was written at Camp David in Maryland, U.S.A. Former American president, Jimmy Carter, helped the two country's leaders come to the agreement in 1978.

Sham el Naseem

Sham el Naseem is Arabic for "sniff the breeze." It is a festival that celebrates the beginning of spring. A national holiday for all Egyptians, it falls on the Monday after Easter, sometime within the month of April or May. In Egypt, Coptic Christians celebrate Easter, but it is not a national holiday.

Coptic Christians attend church on Sham el Naseem. This church in Cairo, called Saint Virgin Mary's Coptic Orthodox Church, is one of the oldest churches in Egypt.

In the morning of Sham el Naseem, many Egyptians head to parks and meadows to enjoy the spring breeze and share a picnic lunch with family and friends. Painting eggs with bright colors or patterns is also a favorite Sham el Naseem tradition, much like the Easter tradition in many places around the world.

Long ago, ancient Egyptians offered salted fish, lettuce, and onions to their gods during Sham el Nassem. Today, Egyptians eat a meal that often includes these foods.

Brightly colored eggs are a symbol of spring and that new life is about to begin.

Labor Day

Labor Day is a holiday that is celebrated in many countries throughout the world. It honors the work that people do. In Egypt, Labor Day falls on May 1. Businesses, offices, and schools are closed for Labor Day. People get to enjoy the time off to spend with their family or friends.

Labor Day is a time to remember and honor the people who work hard every day.

Many other countries, such as the United Kingdom and France, celebrate Labor Day on May 1, too. Some countries celebrate Labor Day on different dates. Canada and the United States celebrate Labor Day on the first Monday in September.

Did You Know?
Labor Day is sometimes called May Day or International Workers' Day. Thousands of years ago, May Day was celebrated as an ancient festival that marked the beginning of spring.

Egyptians enjoy their day off from work and school by spending it with family and friends.

Eid el-Galaa

Eid el-Galaa is a holiday that honors the day that the last British forces left Egypt. It is held on June 18. Eid el-Galaa is sometimes called Evacuation Day. Evacuation means to leave.

Many people wave Egypt's national flag on Evacuation Day.

Items displaying Egypt's national colors can be seen throughout Egypt on Eid el-Galaa.

Great Britain occupied, or moved in to control, Egypt during World War I. In the Egyptian **Revolution** of 1952, Egyptians forced British troops out of Egypt. The country finally gained its **independence** from Great Britain on June 18, 1956. Egyptians celebrate their independence by going to government ceremonies.

Revolution Day

Revolution Day is a national holiday in Egypt. It is held every year on July 23 to mark the **anniversary** of the Egyptian Revolution of 1952. Muhammad Naguib was the leader of the revolution which forced British troops to leave Egypt. King Farouk was overthrown from power and Egypt became an independent **republic**. Muhammad Naguib then became Egypt's first president in 1953.

While Muhammad Naguib was declared the leader of the revolution, Abdel Nasser was really the force behind it. He became Egypt's second president and is honored by Egyptians on Revolution Day.

Egyptians celebrate Revolution Day with concerts and parades. Buildings are decorated with colorful lights, and families and friends get together to share large meals. Many Egyptians gather to hear a speech praising the revolution by the current Egyptian president.

Egypt's new president, Mohamed Morsi, will give the Revolution Day speech in 2012.

Armed Forces Day

Armed Forces Day is a holiday that honors Egyptian men and women who have served in the military. It is held every year on October 6, the date when the October War began in 1973. On that day, Egyptian armed forces attempted to take the Sinai Peninsula back from Israel.

Some Egyptians visit the October War Panorama in Cairo on Armed Forces Day. This memorial features a 3-D mural and a detailed description of Egypt's victories in the 1973 October War.

Many Egyptians enjoy Armed Forces Day by watching a parade. Soldiers march and carry colored flags. Air shows are held for people to watch, too. Air force soldiers perform special flying formations in the air and do stunts.

Military jets perform with colored smoke over the Nile River in Cairo on Armed Forces Day.

Glossary

ancestor A relative from a person's distant past

ancient Very old; dating back thousands of years ago

anniversary The annual date marking an important event

fast To go without eating for a long period of time

independence Freedom from the control of another country

Islamic calendar A calendar used by Muslims that is based on the cycles of the Moon

Jesus Believed by Christians to be the son of God

liberation To be set free

mosque A religious building where Muslims worship

national Related to a nation or country

obedience Willingness to obey someone

pagan A religion that has many different gods

peace treaty A written document that promises a new understanding between two countries so that fighting will stop

prophet Someone who relays God's messages

public Related to the people or citizens of a country

republic A form of government where the people elect their leaders

revolution When people from a country fight against their leader for a change in government

tradition A group of people's shared beliefs and customs that are handed down from the past

Index